Teaching Guide

Specific answers are given as part of this guide. There will be some instances where the answers could vary. If a student has an answer that is reasonable, accept it. The idea of these word puzzles is not only to increase the students' vocabularies, but to also increase their reasoning skills.

Answer Key

Page 1
Across
3. dentist
7. carpenter
9. chemist
10. florist
11. teacher
12. nurse

Down
1. painter
2. pilot
4. lion trainer
5. tailor
6. artist
8. goalie

Page 2
Across
3. grandmother
8. brother
10. sister
11. niece

Down
1. cousin
2. me
4. aunt
5. husband
6. father
7. mother
9. wife

Page 3

```
E H (H E A R I N G) M A M D X
(T) A R M V F H E L A R Y U V
(A) E (T) W S M E L (E A R) S R P
(S) R (O) U E M A I E A T B A S
(T) E (N) W S E G G L W R C O M
(I) K (G) G H S (E Y E) I F L (S) R
(N) G (U) P T T O E I L N E (E) A
(G) I (E) N (F E E L I N G) B (E) D
D F G L I S T O U G S J (I) M
H (F I N G E R) Q U E M O (N) H
O Q E S F S C U V S (N) K (G) T
D A (S M E L L I N G) (O) R E W
V E S A N I C O D U (S) A R E
E C O F U D Y W L H (E) S A M
```

Page 4
Across
1. Martin
5. black
6. equal
8. shot
9. jail
10. minister

Down
2. Alabama
3. peaceful
4. schools
7. Georgia

Page 5
1. Campers use this shelter. - tent
2. Farm animals live in this. - barn
3. An igloo is made of blocks of snow.
4. A king lives in a castle
5. Indians used buffalo skin and poles to make a tepee.
6. Pioneers built log cabins.
7. This shelter has a grass roof. - hut
8. People stay here on vacation. - hotel
9. A small house made of stone or brick is a cottage.
10. Long ago people lived in a cave.

Page 6
Row 1
Title: Jack and Jill
Change: add pail
Title: Humpty Dumpty
Change: fence to wall
Title: Goldilocks
Change: child bear smaller
Row 2
Title: Old Woman Who Lived in a Shoe
Change: house to shoe
Title: Old Mother Hubbard
Change: no bone, cat to dog
Title: Little Red Riding Hood
Change: grandfather to grandmother
Row 3
Title: Ba Ba Black Sheep
Change: white sheep to black
Title: Little Miss Muffet
Change: high chair to stool
Title: Little Jack Horner
Change: table to corner

Page 7

4. (across) mouth
3. (down) strings
6. (down) handle
2. (down) arm
9. (across) gate
5. (down) oar

1. (across) stamp
10. (across) plug
3. (across) shadow
8. (across) net
7. (down) blade
11. (across) sleeve

Page 8

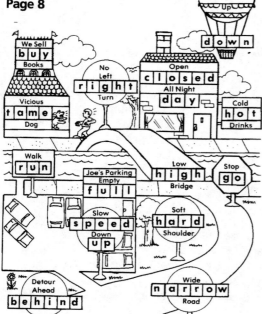

Page 9

Across
1. Pisa
6. White House
9. Capitol
10. Vernon

Down
2. Arch
3. Liberty
4. Gate
5. Monument
7. Palace
8. Empire

Page 10

Row 1 - chili, ice cream
Row 2 - soup, hot dog
Row 3 - cookies, popcorn
Row 4 - milk, pretzels
Row 5 - salad, tacos
Row 6 - fruit, pizza

Page 11

Across
1. stable
4. sap
5. daughter
7. eye
8. arm
10. indians
11. team

Down
2. leg
3. oar
4. sea
5. day
6. herd
8. ant
9. mice

Page 12

```
B A S H F U I A T S C F X
F R G L A S S T Z E O O A
S T R O T O A E O K T O S
T R W O S O M M G O T R R
M U S O O W L E A T H E R
S B S W O O M T P A N E B
R B B T S O H A N H R D W
A E L B C L A L S A A L O
E R U S O N R H P C P E O
P B W A T E R A A I P T D
Y B A A T M T R I T E M R
T U X B O R R Y A R R E P
D R L V N A Y I P A P E R
```

Page 13

1. comb
2. tulip
3. yard
4. swims
5. pillow

6. clock
7. wow
8. chair
9. wow, mom
10. tops, spot

Page 14

Across
1. sad
4. happy
8. brave
10. ashamed
12. temper
13. ignored

Down
2. daydreaming
3. shy
5. idea
6. clumsy
7. red
9. watch
11. help

Page 15

Possible answers:

heat
cut
cud
core
care
con
can
hate
hat
hut
hot
tad
dud
ran

dad
rod
rude
run
rule
race
rot
tan
ton
toad
tore
trace
trade
dear

Page 16

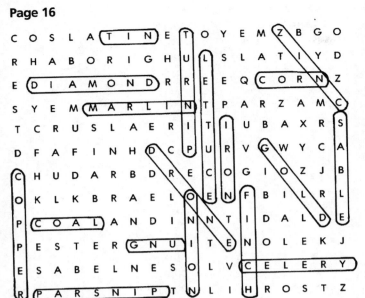

Page 17

Row 1 - pleasant, witty
Row 2 - attractive, immense
Row 3 - forlorn, rapid
Row 4 - content, grin
Row 5 - clever, detest
Row 6 - filthy, annoyed
Row 7 - dull, grand
Row 8 - still, naughty

Page 18

1. D
2. G
3. L
4. A
5. F
6. E
7. K
8. H
9. J
10. C
11. H
12. I

Page 19

hand, neck, foot, ear, back, finger, face
nose, knee, eye, elbow, head, bone, feet

Page 20

1. right
2. tired
3. even
4. glad
5. polite
6. odd
7. nervous
8. stop
9. useful
10. calm
11. timid
12. quiet
13. brave
14. tired
15. swift
16. noble
17. dirty
18. kindly

Page 21

Across
1. left

Down
2. fly

Page 21 (Cont.)

Across
3. stick
4. hail
6. loaf
7. yard
11. swallow
14. tip
15. miss
16. mine

Down
3. story
4. hide
5. lock
8. date
9. bark
10. pupil
11. slip
12. lead
13. wind

Page 22

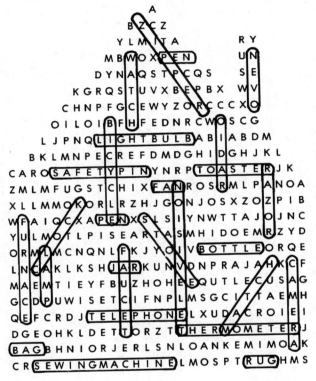

Page 23

Across
1. water
3. say
5. pilot
7. bird
9. on
11. in
13. sea
14. eye
16. dry
17. read
19. artist
23. won
24. sheep

Down
2. thirsty
4. arm
5. plane
6. oar
8. bear
10. he
12. nest
15. odd
18. die
20. tree
21. sour
22. go

Page 24

1. beach
2. ocean
3. (across) dough
3. (down) Denver
4. goose
5. south
6. Boston
7. twenty
8. coach
9. toe
10. (across) seed
10. (down) ship
11. north
12. July
13. pal
14. lark
15. sir

Page 25

See page for diagram.

Page 25 (Cont.)

First pyramid
A
an
can
scan
scant

Second pyramid
I
it
pit
spit
spite

Third pyramid
O
on
one
bone
boner

Page 26

1. great, grate
2. tail, tale
3. led, lead
4. dew, do
5. way, weigh
6. your, you're
7. road, rode
8. dough, doe
9. hour, our
10. right, write
11. through, threw
12. hair, hare
13. red, read
14. days, daze
15. sum, some
16. meat, meet
17. two, to
18. would, wood
19. dear, deer
20. ring, wring

Page 27

Column 1	Column 2
too	cat
two	pat
won	pet
jaw	boy
jar	joy
ear	jay
face	cry
race	fry
rack	far
jack	fan
nest	mint
neat	pint
seat	pine
heat	pane
chop	hat
shop	hot
soup	not
sour	now

Page 28

Help Wanted

WORD BOX

artist
carpenter
chemist
dentist
florist
goalie
lion trainer
nurse
painter
pilot
tailor
teacher

ACROSS
3   7   9   10   11   12

DOWN
1   2   4   5   6   8

Family Tree

me · mother · father · brother · sister · nephew · husband · wife · niece · cousin · aunt · uncle · grandmother · grandfather

ACROSS

3. Your father's mother is your _____.
8. Your mother's son is your _____.
10. Your aunt is your mother's _____.
11. Your aunt's daughter is your mother's _____.

DOWN

1. Your dad's nephew is your _____.
2. This is one of my parent's children.
4. Your mother's sister is your _____.
5. Your father is your mother's _____.
6. Your mother's husband is your _____.
7. Your sister's mother is your _____.
9. Your mother is your father's _____.

A Lot of Sense

You'll find five senses in the letters below. Circle them quickly. Ready-set-go! The words read across or down.

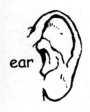

ear

eye

feeling

finger

nose

seeing

smell

taste

tongue

```
E  H  H  E  A  R  I  N  G  M  A  M  D  X
T  A  R  M  V  F  H  E  L  A  R  Y  U  V
A  E  T  W  S  M  E  L  E  A  R  S  R  P
S  R  O  U  E  M  A  I  E  A  T  B  A  S
T  E  N  W  S  E  G  G  L  W  R  C  O  M
I  K  G  G  H  S  E  Y  E  I  F  L  S  R
N  G  U  P  T  T  O  E  I  L  N  E  E  A
G  I  E  N  F  E  E  L  I  N  G  B  E  D
D  F  G  L  I  S  T  O  U  N  S  J  I  M
H  F  I  N  G  E  R  Q  U  E  M  O  N  H
O  Q  E  S  F  S  C  U  V  S  N  K  G  T
D  A  S  M  E  L  L  I  N  G  O  R  E  W
V  E  S  A  N  I  C  O  D  U  S  A  R  E
E  C  O  F  U  D  Y  W  L  H  E  S  A  M
```

hearing

To use these five senses,
You'll need certain things.
Go back to the letters,
And make five more rings.

MP3448 Word Puzzlers

Martin Luther King

WORD BOX

Alabama	black	equal
Georgia	jail	Martin
minister	peaceful	schools
	shot	

ACROSS

1. _____ Luther King was a great leader.

5. He helped _____ people in many ways.

6. He worked hard so that people would have _____ rights.

8. Martin Luther King was _____ and killed on April 4, 1968.

9. Many people thought he broke the law and had him put in _____.

10. After he finished college, he became a _____.

DOWN

2. King lived in Montgomery _____.

3. Martin Luther begged people to act in a _____ way.

4. King wanted children to have better _____.

7. Martin Luther King was born in Atlanta, _____.

Homes

Study each sentence to figure out how the words have been changed. All words have been changed in the same way.

barn

tent

hotel

cave

1. AMPERSC SEU HIST HELTERS. _____

_____

2. ARMF NIMALSA IVEL NI HIST. _____

_____

3. NA _____ SI ADEM FO LOCKSB FO NOWS.

_____

4. A INGK IVESL NI A _____.

_____

igloo

5. NDIANSI SEDU UFFALOB KINS NDA OLESP OT
AKEM A _____.

cottage

_____

6. IONEERSP UILTB _____.

_____

castle

7. HIST HELTERS ASH A RASSG OOFR. _____

_____

8. EOPLEP TAYS EREH NO ACATIONV. _____

_____

tent

9. A MALLS OUSEH ADEM FO TONES RO RICKB
SI A _____.

_____

log cabin

10. ONGL GOA EOPLEP IVEDL NI A _____.

hut

_____

Puzzling Nursery Rhymes

In each picture below, a nursery rhyme has something wrong in it. Study each picture carefully. Name the nursery rhyme and what needs to be changed.

Title:_____

Change:_____

Title:_____

Change:_____

Title:_____

Change:_____

Title:_____

Change:_____

Title:_____

Change:_____

Title:_____

Change:_____

Title:_____

Change:_____

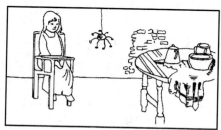

Title:_____

Change:_____

Title:_____

Change:_____

Look Here!

Study each picture carefully. In the correct place in the puzzle, write the word that tells what is missing in each picture.

4 Across

3 Down

6 Down

2 Down

9 Across

5 down

1 Across

10 Across

3 Across

8 Across

7 Down

11 Across

Antonym City

Welcome to Antonym City, U.S.A. Write an antonym (an opposite) for each word in the space provided.

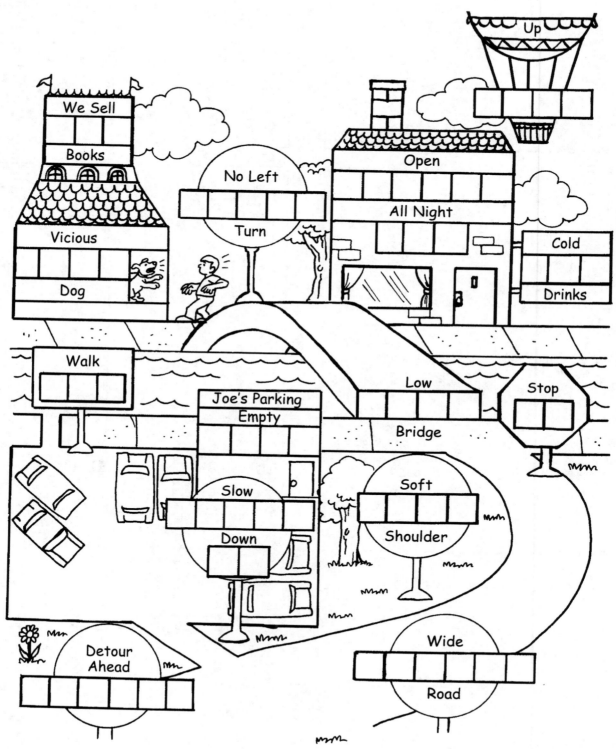

Monuments & Buildings

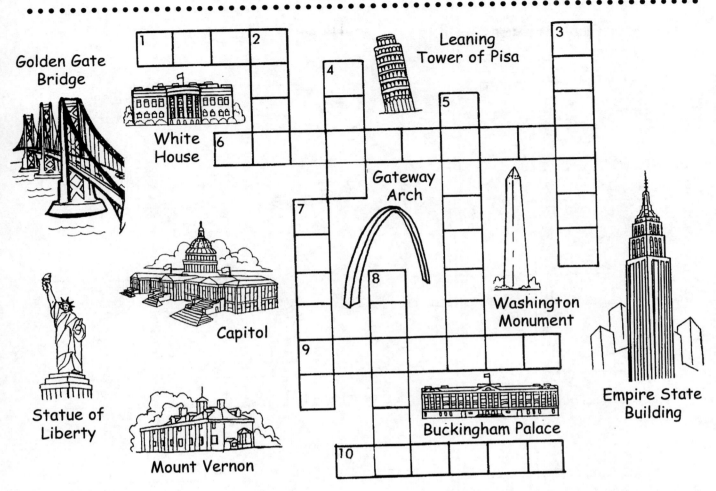

Golden Gate Bridge

White House

Leaning Tower of Pisa

Gateway Arch

Washington Monument

Capitol

Statue of Liberty

Mount Vernon

Buckingham Palace

Empire State Building

ACROSS

1. I am a famous building in Italy. I am the Leaning Tower of _____.
6. Many famous men have lived here. It is the home of the President of the United States.
9. I am the building on which Congress meets. I have a beautiful dome.
10. Mount _____ was the home of George Washington.

DOWN

2. I am 630 feet high and I'm made of stainless steel. I am called the Gateway _____.

3. I am in the New York Harbor. I carry a torch and wear a crown. I am the Statue of _____.
4. One of the largest bridges in the world is in San Francisco. It is the Golden _____ Bridge.
5. I am in the United States capitol. I look like a huge needle. I am the Washington _____.
7. I am the home of the Queen of England. I am Buckingham _____.
8. One of the world's tallest skyscrapers is in New York City. It is the _____ State Building.

   MP3448 Word Puzzlers

What's for Lunch?

Can you unscramble the signs in the school cafeteria?

LICHI ☐☐☐☐☐

CEI RMECA ☐☐☐ ☐☐☐☐☐

PSUO ☐☐☐☐

HTO GDO ☐☐☐ ☐☐☐

KCEISOO ☐☐☐☐☐☐☐

PCOONRP ☐☐☐☐☐☐☐

LMIK ☐☐☐☐

ZPTLRSEE ☐☐☐☐☐☐☐☐

LDAAS ☐☐☐☐☐

CTOAS ☐☐☐☐☐

TUFRI ☐☐☐☐☐

ZAIZP ☐☐☐☐☐

Analogies

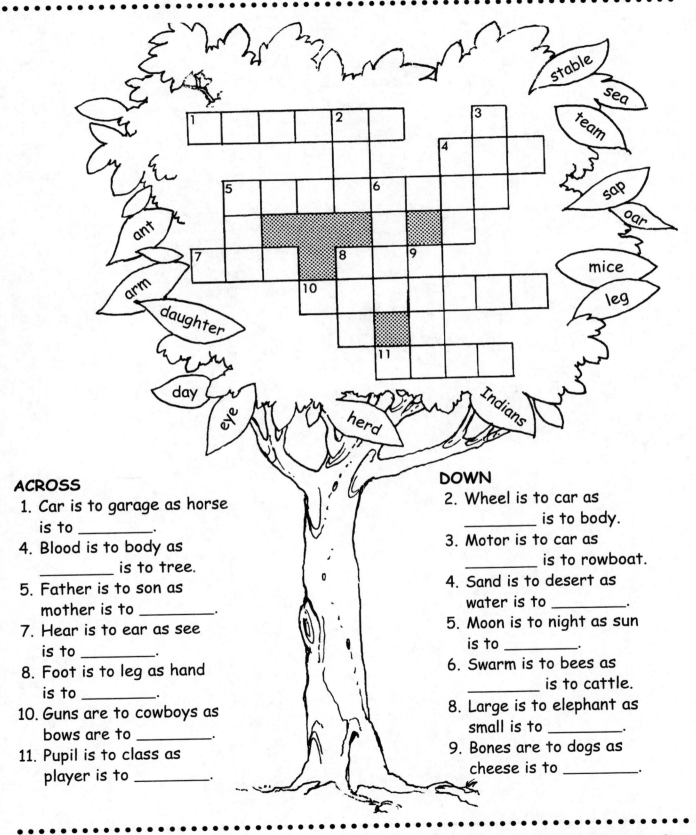

ACROSS

1. Car is to garage as horse is to _____.
4. Blood is to body as _____ is to tree.
5. Father is to son as mother is to _____.
7. Hear is to ear as see is to _____.
8. Foot is to leg as hand is to _____.
10. Guns are to cowboys as bows are to _____.
11. Pupil is to class as player is to _____.

DOWN

2. Wheel is to car as _____ is to body.
3. Motor is to car as _____ is to rowboat.
4. Sand is to desert as water is to _____.
5. Moon is to night as sun is to _____.
6. Swarm is to bees as _____ is to cattle.
8. Large is to elephant as small is to _____.
9. Bones are to dogs as cheese is to _____.

MP3448 Word Puzzlers

How do You Make it?

cotton

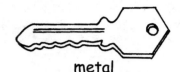

metal

wool

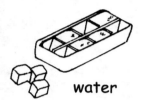

water

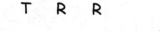

glass

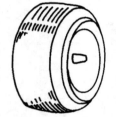

rubber

leather

paper

wax

wood

```
B  A  S  H  F  U  I  A  T  S  C  F  X
F  R  G  L  A  S  S  T  Z  E  O  O  A
S  T  R  O  T  O  A  E  O  K  T  O  S
T  R  W  O  S  O  M  M  G  O  T  R  R
M  U  S  O  O  W  L  E  A  T  H  E  R
S  B  S  W  O  O  M  T  P  A  N  E  B
R  B  B  T  S  O  H  A  N  H  R  D  W
A  E  L  B  C  L  A  L  S  A  A  L  O
E  R  U  S  O  N  R  H  P  C  P  E  O
P  B  W  A  T  E  R  A  A  I  P  T  D
Y  B  A  A  T  M  T  R  I  T  E  M  R
T  U  X  B  O  R  R  Y  A  R  R  E  P
D  R  L  V  N  A  Y  I  P  A  P  E  R
```

To make these items,
What would you use?
In the puzzle above,
You'll find your clues.
The words read across or down.

Riddles, Riddles

Find the answers to the riddles in the tail of the kite. The letters for each answer are in order in the kite for each word.

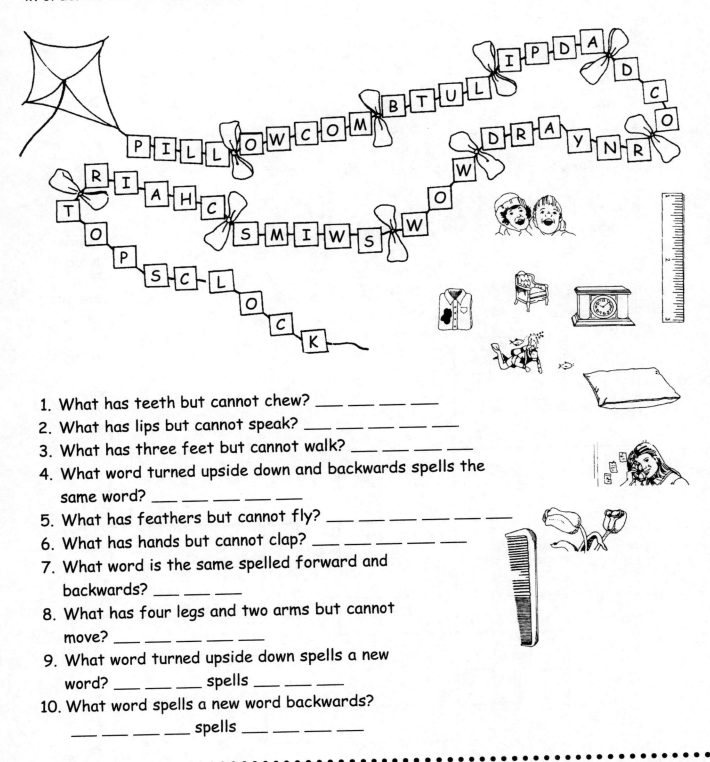

1. What has teeth but cannot chew? ___ ___ ___ ___

2. What has lips but cannot speak? ___ ___ ___ ___ ___

3. What has three feet but cannot walk? ___ ___ ___ ___

4. What word turned upside down and backwards spells the same word? ___ ___ ___ ___ ___

5. What has feathers but cannot fly? ___ ___ ___ ___ ___

6. What has hands but cannot clap? ___ ___ ___ ___ ___

7. What word is the same spelled forward and backwards? ___ ___ ___

8. What has four legs and two arms but cannot move? ___ ___ ___ ___

9. What word turned upside down spells a new word? ___ ___ ___ spells ___ ___ ___

10. What word spells a new word backwards? ___ ___ ___ ___ spells ___ ___ ___ ___

MP3448 Word Puzzlers

Use an Idiom!

Find the word below which matches each idiom and complete the puzzle.

ACROSS

1. I really feel down in the dumps.
   I am _____.
4. She is walking on air.
   She is _____ .
8. When you keep your chin up, you are being _____.
10. She is hanging her head. She is _____.
12. He blew his top. He lost his _____.
13. He gave me the cold shoulder. He _____ me.

DOWN

2. He's got his head in the clouds. He is _____.
3. The cat's got her tongue. She is _____ .
5. She has a bee in her bonnet. She has an _____.
6. He is really a butter-fingers. He is _____.
7. She is a carrot top. Her hair is _____.
9. Keep an eye on the baby means to _____ him.
11. If you lend a friend a hand, you will _____ him.

shy
help
ashamed
brave
clumsy
daydreaming
happy
idea
ignored
red
sad
watch
temper

Moving Letters

The Letterbugs move around to form words such as

How many words can you find by moving the Letterbugs?

Here are the rules for moving the Letterbugs to form words:

1. A word must have two or more letters.
2. Each letter may be used in any word.
3. No letter may be used more than one time in a word.
4. No other letters of the alphabet may be used.

Words from Letterbugs

heat			
			✱

✱ Continue on another paper if necessary.

Seek, Find, and Classify

Place each word listed below in the correct category at the bottom of the page.
Then find and circle each word in the square of letters. The words can read down,
across, or diagonally.

parsnip	iron	sable	diamond	corn	zinc
drone	gold	onion	turnip	coal	finch
copper	celery	tin	gnu	lettuce	marlin

```
C  O  S  L  A  T  I  N  E  T  O  Y  E  M  Z  B  G  O
R  H  A  B  O  R  I  G  H  U  L  S  L  A  T  I  Y  D
E  D  I  A  M  O  N  D  R  R  E  E  Q  C  O  R  N  Z
S  Y  E  M  M  A  R  L  I  N  T  P  A  R  Z  A  M  C
T  C  R  U  S  L  A  E  R  I  T  I  U  B  A  X  R  S
D  F  A  F  I  N  H  D  C  P  U  R  V  G  W  Y  C  A
C  H  U  D  A  R  B  D  R  E  C  O  G  I  O  Z  J  B
O  K  L  K  B  R  A  E  L  O  E  N  F  B  I  L  R  L
P  C  O  A  L  A  N  D  I  N  N  T  I  D  A  L  D  E
P  E  S  T  E  R  G  N  U  I  T  E  N  O  L  E  K  J
E  S  A  B  E  L  N  E  S  O  L  V  C  E  L  E  R  Y
R  P  A  R  S  N  I  P  T  N  L  I  H  R  O  S  T  Z
```

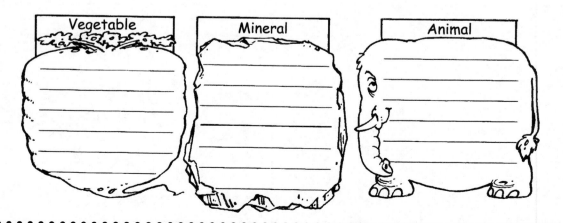

Vegetable

Mineral

Animal

Hieroglyphic Word Exchange

Using the key provided, write a letter beneath each symbol in the puzzle below to spell more colorful synonyms for the words listed. The first one has been done for you.

HIEROGLYPHIC KEY

a	b	c	d	e	f	g	h	i	j	k	l	m

n	o	p	q	r	s	t	u	v	w	x	y	z

nice   p l e a s a n t

cute   _ _ _ _ _ _ _ _ _ _

sad   _ _ _ _ _ _ _

happy   _ _ _ _ _ _ _ _

smart   _ _ _ _ _ _

dirty   _ _ _ _ _ _ _ _

dumb   _ _ _ _ _

quiet   _ _ _ _ _ _ _

funny   _ _ _ _ _ _

large   _ _ _ _ _ _ _

fast   _ _ _ _ _

smile   _ _ _ _

hate   _ _ _ _ _ _ _

mad   _ _ _ _ _ _ _

great   _ _ _ _ _ _

bad   _ _ _ _ _ _ _ _

MP3448 Word Puzzlers

Analogy Puzzles

Study the first two drawings to see how they are alike. Then look at the third drawing and find a drawing in the Puzzle Box that is alike in the same way and fill in the blank with the letter of the correct drawing. The first two have been completed for you.

⊂ is to ⊃ as ⊃ is to _____1_____.

◯ is to ▷ as ▢ is to _____2_____.

PUZZLE BOX

1. ▢ is to ▫ as ◯ is to _____.

2. ▢ is to ◯ as ◰ is to _____.

3. ▦ is to ⊕ as ▭ is to _____.

4. ⌇ is to S as ⊐ is to _____.

5. ◰ is to ▤ as ◔ is to _____.

6. ▯ is to ▭ as ▯ is to _____.

7. ◙ is to ▣ as △◯ is to _____.

8. ▦ is to ⊕ as ▫▫ / ▫▫ is to _____.

9. ▢ is to ▯ as ◯ is to _____.

10. ◩ is to ■ as ◸ is to _____.

11. ⊟ is to ° as ▦ is to _____.

12. ▢° is to ▢△ as △▢ is to _____.

PUZZLE BOX	
Example 1	Example 2
⊃	▯
A. E	I. ▢◦
B. ⊕	J. ☾
C. ◢	K. ⊿◯
D. ◦	L. ⊖
E. ▱	
F. ⊕	
G. ⊘	
H. ◦◦ / ◦◦	

Around the Circle

Find fifteen body parts hidden in these circles. Choose a letter from the outside circle. Then try to spell a word by moving to the next circle. You must follow the circles in order.

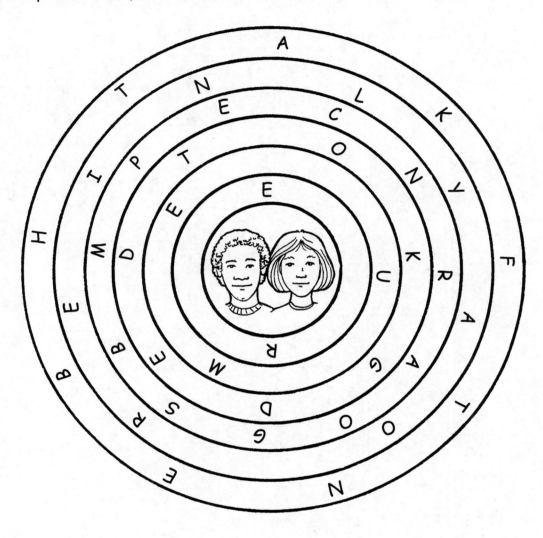

ARM _____

_____

_____

_____

_____

Definitions for Detectives

Use the definitions and the number code to figure out each synonym. Write the letters in the correct place in the acrostic.

CODE

1 = Z	
2 = A	
3 = Y	
4 = B	
5 = X	
6 = C	
7 = W	
8 = D	
9 = V	
10 = E	
11 = U	
12 = F	
13 = T	
14 = G	
15 = S	
16 = H	
17 = R	
18 = I	
19 = M	
20 = J	
21 = P	
22 = K	
23 = O	
24 = L	
25 = N	
26 = Q	

1. correct
2. sleepy
3. smooth
4. happy
5. courteous
6. unusual
7. jittery
8. quit
9. helpful
10. peaceful
11. shy
12. still
13. heroic
14. exhausted
15. rapid
16. great
17. unclean
18. agreeable

G 17 18 __ 16 13

R 13 18 __ 10 8

E 10 9 __ 25

A 14 24 __ 8

T 21 23 24 18 __ 10

D 23 __ 8

E 25 __ 17 9 23 11 15

T 15 __ 23 21

E 11 15 __ 12 11 24

C __ 2 24 19

T __ 18 19 18 8

I 26 11 __ 10 13

V 4 17 2 __ 10

E 13 18 17 __ 8

W 15 __ 18 12 13

O 25 __ 4 24 10

R 8 18 __ 13 3

K __ 18 25 8 24 3

Homograms: Two for One

Homograms are words that look alike but have different meanings. Study the two meanings given for each word. Write the word in the correct squares in the puzzle.

ACROSS

1. direction
   did leave
3. thin piece of wood
   pierce
4. piece of ice from the sky
   shout of welcome
6. shape of bread
   to do nothing, be idle
7. 36 inches
   space around a house
11. a kind of bird
    take in water
14. end point
    money for a service
15. unmarried girl
    fail to hit
16. hole in the ground for ore
    belonging to me

DOWN

2. insect
   move through the air
3. floor of a building
   series of happenings
4. keep out of sight
   skin of an animal
5. a curl of hair
   fasten the door
8. day, week, month
   a kind of fruit
9. a tree skin
   sound of a dog
10. a student
    part of an eye
11. a small piece of paper
    to slide accidentally
12. to show the way
    a metal
13. to turn
    air in motion

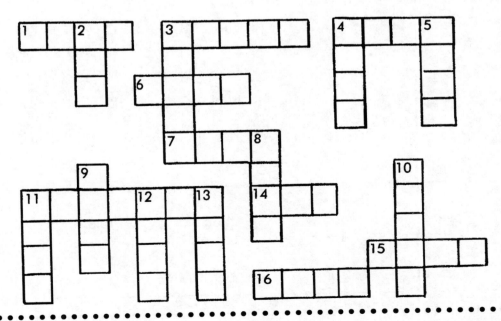

MP3448 Word Puzzlers

Inventions in a Home

The word search contains inventions found in a home. Find and circle each invention in the word box. The words can read down, up, across, and diagonally.

```
                    A
                  B Z C Z
                Y L M I T A              R Y
                M B W O X P E N           U N
                  D Y N A Q S T P C Q S     S E
              K G R Q S T U V X B E P B X   W V
            C H N P F G C E W Y Z O R C C C X O
          O I L O I B F H F E D N R C W O S C G
        L J P N Q L I G H T B U L B A B I A B D M
      B K L M N P E C R E F D M D G H I D G H J K L
    C A R O S A F E T Y P I N Y N R P T O A S T E R J K
    Z M L M F U G S T C H I X F A N R O S R M L P A N O A
    X L L M M O K O R L R Z H J G O N J O S X Z O Z P I B
    W F A I Q C X A P E N X S L S I Y N W T T A J O J N C
    Y U L M O T L P I S E A R T A S M H I D O E M R Z Y D
    O R M L M C N Q N L F K J Y O I V B O T T L E O R Q E
    L N C A K L K S H J A R K U N V D N P R A J A H K C F
    M A E M T I E Y F B U Z H O H E E Q U T L E C U S A G
    G C D P U W I S E T C I F N P L M S G C I T T A E M H
    Q E F C R D J T E L E P H O N E L X U D A C R O I E I
    D G E O H K L D E T T O R Z T T H E R M O M E T E R J
    B A G B H N I O R J E R L S N L O A N K E M I M O A K
    C R S E W I N G M A C H I N E L M O S P T R U G H M S
```

WORD BOX

toaster	jar	clock	safety pin	bicycle	radio
telephone	oven	fan	faucet	television	stove
thermometer	camera	bottle	lamp	sewing machine	lock
watch	furnace	match	pen	razor	zipper
	light bulb	rug	bag		

Analogies

Analogies are similarities between things. In this puzzle, the analogies are between the pairs of words in the statements. Choose the word that best completes each analogy and finish the puzzle.

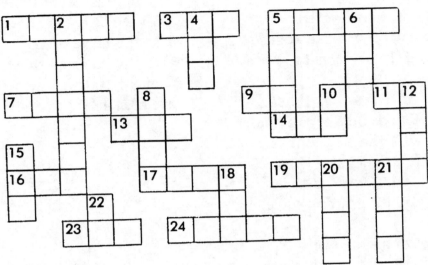

ACROSS

1. Bird is to sky as fish is to __ __ __ __ __.
3. Ear is to hear as mouth is to __ __ __.
5. Car is to driver as airplane is to __ __ __ __ __.
7. Fur is to squirrel as feather is to __ __ __ __.
9. Skinny is to fat as off is to __ __.
11. Cold is to hot as out is to __ __.
13. Sand is to desert as water is to __ __ __.
14. Radio is to ear as book is to __ __ __.
16. Swamp is to wet as desert is to __ __ __.
17. Voice is to sing as eye is to __ __ __ __.
19. Poem is to poet as painting is to __ __ __ __ __ __.
23. Pail is to pale as one is to __ __ __.
24. Hair is to dog as wool is to __ __ __ __.

DOWN

2. Food is to hungry as water is to __ __ __ __ __ __ __.
4. Foot is to leg as hand is to __ __ __.
5. Garage is to car as hangar is to __ __ __ __ __.
6. Motor is to car as __ __ __ is to rowboat.
8. Calf is to cow as cub is to __ __ __ __.
10. She is to her as __ __ is to him.
12. Spider is to web as bird is to __ __ __ __.
15. Two is to even as three is to __ __ __.
18. Push is to pull as live is to __ __ __.
20. Rose is to plant as oak is to __ __ __ __.
21. Orange is to sweet as lemon is to __ __ __ __.
22. Begin is to end as stop is to __ __.

MP3448 Word Puzzlers

Following Directions

1. If Florida is a state, write beach. If it is an island, write sandy.

2. If an ocean is larger than a sea, write ocean. If it is not, write water.

3. (Across) If your mother bakes bread doe, write bread. If she cannot, write dough.

3. (Down) Look at the names of these cities: Boston, Biloxi, Denver, Toledo. Write the name of the city that is west of the Mississippi.

4. Write moose if 2 1/2 is more than 2 2/4. If 2 1/2 and 2 2/4 are equal, write goose.

5. If Canada is south of the North Pole, write south. If it is not, write north.

6. Write the name of the city from the list in 3 Down which is closest to the Atlantic Ocean.

7. Now write the largest of these numbers:
   twenty   fifteen   thirteen

8. If there are eleven men on a football team, write coach. If there are not, write field.

9. If a clog and a sandal are worn on the feet, write toe. If they are not, write eye.

10. (Across) If you sow seed, write seed. If you do not, write seam.

10. (Down) Write milk if you would buy a galleon of milk. If you would not, write ship.

11. If Canada is south of the equator, write south. If it is not, write north.

12. What month has a first, a second, and a third but is most famous for its fourth?

13. Be sure to write pal if an ally is a friend. If it is not, write foe.

14. Look at these words: LARK   CARP. If 8 x 9 + 3 is the same as 3 x 25, write the name of the bird. If it is not, write the name of the fish.

15. If knight follows day, write day in the puzzle. If not, write sir.

Word Diamond

Color the words blue that show action. Color the words red that show feeling. Color the words yellow that show a person or thing.

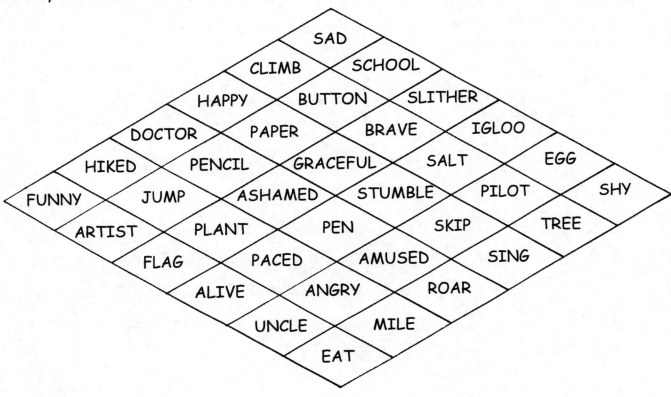

Can you build a pyramid of words? Add a letter to each line to form a new word.

___	first letter of alphabet	— me
___ ___	an article	___ ___ a thing
___ ___ ___	could	___ ___ ___ a deep hole
___ ___ ___ ___	look at	___ ___ ___ ___ saliva from mouth
___ ___ ___ ___ ___	barely enough	___ ___ ___ ___ ___ grudge

          ___   looks like zero
        ___ ___   opposite of off
     ___ ___ ___   three minus two
  ___ ___ ___ ___   part of the skeleton
___ ___ ___ ___ ___   foolish mistake; blunder

Homophone Chains

This chain contains twenty words that have a HOMOPHONE. Homophones are words that sound alike but are spelled differently, such as ate and eight. The homophones are in order in the chain. The last letter or the last two letters of each word begin a new word. Find each word and write it below. Beneath it, write its homophone from the Word Box.

WORD BOX

read	threw
meet	weigh
tale	daze
to	our
lead	doe
wring	you're
hare	grate
write	wood
rode	some
do	deer

1. _great_
   grate

2. _____

3. _____

4. _____

5. _____

6. _____

7. _____

8. _____

9. _____

10. _____

11. _____

12. _____

13. _____

14. _____

15. _____

16. _____

17. _____

18. _____

19. _____

20. _____

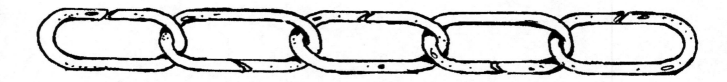

Word-to-Word

Change just one letter at a time in each line in the example shown, and you will change a cent to a dime. In each word-to-word box below, change one letter in each line to form a new word. You may have to rearrange letters.

C	E	N	T
L	E	N	T
L	I	N	T
L	I	N	E
D	I	N	E
D	I	M	E

T	O	O
W	O	N

one plus one

J	A	W
E	A	R

a container

F	A	C	E
J	A	C	K

a contest

a holder

N	E	S	T
H	E	A	T

careful

chair

C	H	O	P

store

kind of food

bitter taste

C	A	T
P	E	T

to touch lightly

B	O	Y
J	A	Y

happiness

C	R	Y
F	A	N

to cook

a long way

M	I	N	T

a measure

kind of tree

piece of glass

H	A	T

warm

never

at this time

MP3448 Word Puzzlers

Postal Abbreviations

When you write a letter, you may use postal abbreviations for each state. Circle the state abbreviations in the puzzle. They may read across, down, and diagonally.

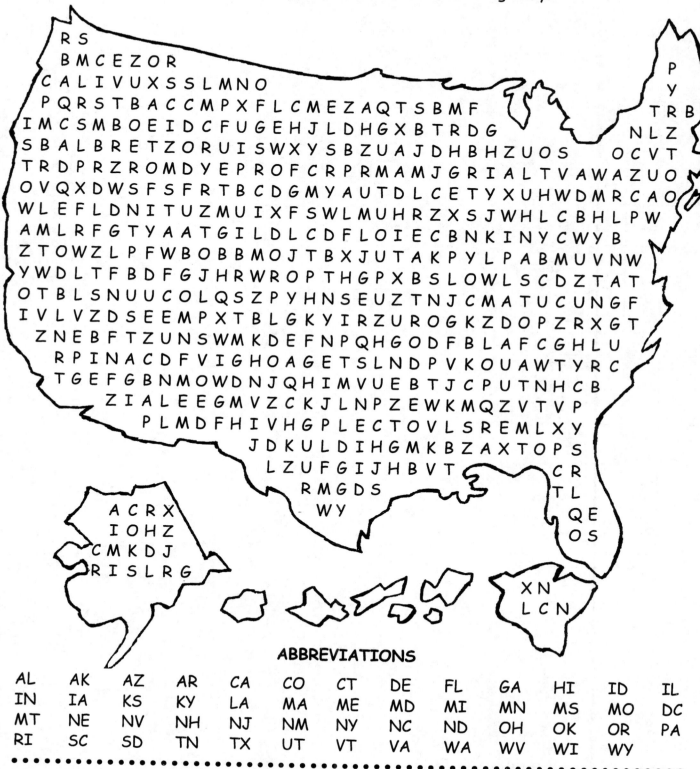

ABBREVIATIONS

AL	AK	AZ	AR	CA	CO	CT	DE	FL	GA	HI	ID	IL
IN	IA	KS	KY	LA	MA	ME	MD	MI	MN	MS	MO	DC
MT	NE	NV	NH	NJ	NM	NY	NC	ND	OH	OK	OR	PA
RI	SC	SD	TN	TX	UT	VT	VA	WA	WV	WI	WY	